The Old Church, Bonchurch by E. W. Haslehust

ISLE OF WIGHT RECIPES

compiled by
Dorothy Baldock
with the assistance of
THE ISLE OF WIGHT COUNTY FEDERATION
OF WOMEN'S INSTITUTES

SALMON

INDEX

Cover pictures: *front:* Godshill by W. W. Quartremain
back: The Needles by A. Heaton Cooper

Printed and Published by J. Salmon Ltd., Sevenoaks, England ©

ISLE OF WIGHT FARMHOUSE CAKE

½ lb. flour
¼ lb. butter or lard
¼ lb. sugar
¼ lb. sultanas
¼ lb. raisins
¼ lb. currants
1 oz. chopped mixed peel
½ teaspoon mixed spice
Pinch of salt
1 medium egg, well beaten
¼ teaspoon bicarbonate of soda
¼ pt. milk
A few slices of peel

Set oven to 350°F or Mark 4 and well grease a 2 lb loaf tin. In a bowl, rub the fat into the flour until it resembles fine breadcrumbs. Add all the dry ingredients except the bicarbonate of soda and mix well. Slightly warm the milk in a pan and add the bicarbonate of soda. Make a well in the centre of the mixture, add the milk and the well-beaten egg and stir thoroughly together. Put the mixture into the loaf tin and arrange a few slices of peel along the top. Bake for 2 to 2½ hours until nicely brown and a skewer pushed into the centre comes out clean. Leave to stand for a few minutes and then turn out on a wire rack to cool.

Sandown Bay by A. Heaton Cooper

SANDOWN PUDDING

10-12 Boudoir biscuits
1 pt. milk
2 tablespoons custard powder
1 tablespoon sugar
1 sachet gelatine
2 oz. glacé cherries
2 oz. Ratafia biscuits

Make up 1 pint of custard in a pan and then remove from the heat. Whisk the gelatine into the very hot, but not boiling, custard and set aside for about half an hour to cool. Meanwhile, take a 6–7 inch cake tin, line the bottom with baking parchment and butter the sides. Cut the boudoir biscuits in half and stand them, sugar side outwards and cut end upwards, around the sides of the cake tin. Arrange the glacé cherries over the bottom of the tin and then cover with the Ratafia biscuits. Carefully pour in the custard mixture; the biscuits will rise to the surface. Put into the refrigerator to set. When required, slightly warm the sides of the tin in hot water, turn out on to a dish, decorate with whipped cream and serve. Serves 6–8.

Vectis Syrup Roll

¼ lb. self-raising flour
2 oz. shredded suet
1 oz. sugar
2 fl.oz. (approx.) water
1 oz. currants
1 medium apple, peeled, cored and finely chopped
Grated rind of ½ lemon
¼ - ½ teaspoon mixed spice
1 tablespoon black treacle or golden syrup

In a bowl, mix together the flour, suet and sugar with sufficient water to make a stiff paste. In a separate bowl, mix together the currants, chopped apple, lemon rind, spice and treacle or syrup. Roll out the pastry thinly (approximately ⅛ inch thick) on a well-floured surface to a rectangle of a width suitable for the steamer available. Spread the mixture evenly over the pastry, leaving a clear strip all round. Roll up, wet the edge and seal, and press down and well seal the ends. Wrap in kitchen foil, leaving room for expansion, and seal well. Steam for 2 hours, topping up the water as necessary. Turn out and serve with custard. Serves 4.

This pudding takes its name from the Roman name for the Isle of Wight – Vectis Insula.

Shorwell by A. Heaton Cooper

Freshwater Bay by W. W. Quartremain

BUTTERED CRAB

1 large boiled crab
1 or 2 small anchovy fillets - these
can be pre-soaked in a little milk
to remove excess saltiness
¼ pint white wine
1 to 1½ oz. fresh white or
brown breadcrumbs
Salt, (if desired), and black pepper
¼ teaspoon grated nutmeg
2 oz. butter
1 teaspoon lemon juice
Parsley sprigs for garnish
Hot buttered toast, cut into triangles

If preferred the crab mixture can be
served spread directly on to the buttered
toast.

Remove the brown and white crab meat from the shell and claws and set aside. Drain the anchovies well, if they have been soaked, and mash well with the wine and breadcrumbs. Add seasoning to taste and the nutmeg. Place the mixture in a saucepan, bring to the boil, stirring, then simmer for 5 minutes, continuing to stir. Remove from the heat. Melt the butter in a pan and stir in the lemon juice. Flake the reserved crab-meat and add to the butter. Stir the crab mixture lightly into the anchovy mixture and cook for a further 3 to 4 minutes. Divide the mixture evenly between four small heated plates, piling it up in the centre, garnish with parsley sprigs and serve, edged with triangles of buttered toast. Serves 4.

OSBORNE PUDDING

3 tin slices of brown bread, very lightly
buttered and the crusts removed
Orange marmalade
½ pint milk
2½ to 3 fl. oz. double cream
4 egg yolks
1½ oz. sugar
1 dessertspoon medium sherry
½ pint whipped cream
Glacé cherries and angelica 'leaves'
for decoration

Spread the slices of bread with marmalade and cut into tiny pieces. Heat the milk and double cream together in a saucepan. Whisk the egg yolks with the sugar and pour over the milk mixture. Blend well and strain. Pour into a double saucepan and cook, stirring, until thickened. Allow to cool slightly, then fold in the brown bread, sherry and whipped cream. Turn into a serving bowl and chill well before serving decorate with glacé cherries and angelica 'leaves' and serve accompanied by pouring cream. Serves 4.

Queen Victoria was very fond of this chilled, luxury version of Bread and Butter Pudding.

Osborne House by A. Heaton Cooper

The Old Village, Shanklin by W. W. Quartremain

Raisin Cake

1 lb. flour
2 teaspoons baking powder
6 oz. butter
8 oz. granulated sugar
Grated rind of half a lemon or
half an orange
12 oz. raisins
2 eggs
7½ fl. oz. milk

Set oven to 325°F or Mark 3. Sift the flour and baking powder together into a bowl, then rub in the butter until the mixture resembles fine breadcrumbs. Stir in the sugar, rind and raisins. Beat the eggs and milk together and stir into the mixture, which should be fairly stiff. Turn into a greased and lined 8 inch round cake tin and bake for 1¼–1½ hours, covering the top with foil if it appears to be browning too quickly. Cool in the tin for 10 minutes then turn out on to a wire rack.

This is an Isle of Wight luncheon cake. Luncheon cakes, traditionally served with wine and fresh fruit, were developed to bridge the gap between breakfast and dinner.

Cowes Pudding

½ pt. milk
2 eggs
10–12 Boudoir biscuits
2 oz. chopped almonds
2 tablespoons caster sugar
½ oz. butter
4–5 drops almond essence

SAUCE:
3 egg yolks
1 tablespoon caster sugar
¼ pt. cream sherry

Grease a 1 pint pudding basin with the butter. Cut each Boudoir biscuit to the depth of the basin and use them to line the basin, cut ends down and sugar side outwards, covering the bottom of the basin with some of the cut-off pieces. Beat together in a bowl the eggs and sugar. Bring the milk to the boil in a pan and add to the egg mixture, stirring thoroughly. Now stir in the chopped almonds and the almond essence. Carefully pour in the custard to fill the bowl, pressing down the biscuits as may be necessary. Cover with kitchen foil and steam for ¾ hour. When ready, let stand for a minute before turning out on to a serving dish. Pour the sauce round the pudding and serve. To make the sauce, put all the ingredients into a saucepan and whisk over the heat until it thickens, but do not allow to boil. Serves 4.

Yachting at Cowes by E. W. Haslehust

Newchurch by A. Heaton Cooper

GARLIC BUTTER AND GARLIC DIP

GARLIC BUTTER
4 oz. butter, softened
2 plump garlic cloves, peeled
½ teaspoon chopped fresh parsley
A squeeze of lemon juice
Salt and black pepper, (if desired)

Beat the butter until extremely soft – but not oily. Crush the garlic cloves either in a garlic press or with the blade of a knife and combine with the butter together with the parsley, lemon juice and seasoning, if desired. Form into a long roll in a piece of greaseproof paper and chill until firm. To serve, cut into ½ inch sections and place on steak, chops, fish etc., or add to baked jacket potatoes or spread on hot French bread.

GARLIC DIP
2 plump garlic cloves, peeled
1 small onion, peeled and very finely chopped
5 fl. oz. soured cream
A squeeze of lemon juice
Salt and black pepper, (if desired)
Chopped fresh parsley or paprika pepper for garnish

Crush the garlic cloves either in a garlic press or with the blade of a knife and combine with the onion, soured cream, lemon juice and seasoning, if desired. Put into a suitable bowl and chill thoroughly. Serve garnished with parsley or paprika as an accompaniment to crudités, crisps etc.

Isle of Wight Doughnuts

2 lb. strong white flour
Pinch of salt
2 oz. butter or lard
4 oz. caster sugar
1 teaspoon allspice
Pinch of ground cloves
Pinch of ground nutmeg
½ pint milk
½ oz. dried yeast
1½ to 2 oz. currants
1 tablespoon sugar
¼ teaspoon cinnamon
Caster sugar mixed with a little ground cinnamon
Oil for frying

These spicy doughnuts have a filling of currants rather than the usual red jam.

Sift the flour and salt together, then rub in the butter or lard until the mixture resembles fine breadcrumbs. Stir in the sugar and spices. Warm the milk, sprinkle over the yeast and leave until frothy. Add to the flour and stir to form a dough. Turn out on to a floured surface and knead until smooth – about 10 minutes. Place in a clean bowl, cover with a clean tea cloth, and leave in a warm place for 1½ hours to rise. Then knock back and knead again. Form into balls the size of a small apple. Mix the currants, sugar and cinnamon together, make a small hole in each doughnut and insert a few currants, then close up. Leave the doughnuts in a warm place for 10 minutes. Heat the oil and deep-fry in small batches, turning once, until golden. Drain well on kitchen paper, then toss in the cinnamon and caster sugar.

Blackgang Chine by A. Heaton Cooper

RYDE FROM THE PIER.

Ryde from the Pier by W. W. Quartremain

CUTLETS VICTORIA

1 lb. white fish, cooked and flaked –
sole, plaice etc.
2 oz. butter
2 oz. flour
½ pint single cream
4 oz. mushrooms, wiped, trimmed and
finely sliced
1 small onion or shallot, peeled and
finely grated
1 heaped dessertspoon fresh,
chopped parsley
1 teaspoon lemon juice
Salt and black pepper
A little flour, seasoned with salt and
black pepper and a pinch of dry
English mustard powder
1 egg, lightly beaten
Crisp, fine breadcrumbs for coating
Fat for frying
Parsley sprigs and lemon wedges
for garnish

Ensure all bones and skin are removed from the flaked fish. Melt the butter in a saucepan, stir in the flour and cook through, stirring. Gradually add the cream, stirring all the time. Add the fish, mushrooms, onion or shallot, parsley, lemon juice and seasoning. Combine well and heat through thoroughly. Remove the mixture from the saucepan and leave to cool. Divide the mixture into eight pieces and shape each piece into a 'cutlet'. Dust with the seasoned flour, then brush with beaten egg and coat evenly with the breadcrumbs. Heat the fat and shallow fry the 'cutlets' until golden. Drain well on kitchen paper. Serve garnished with parsley sprigs and lemon wedges and accompanied by creamed potatoes and green peas. Serves 4.

Half-pay Pudding

2 oz. suet
2 oz. flour
2 oz. fresh breadcrumbs
2 oz. currants
2 oz. raisins
¼ pt milk
1 tablespoon black treacle

Well butter a 1 pint pudding basin. Mix together all the ingredients in a bowl and place into the pudding basin. Cover with greaseproof paper and kitchen foil. Steam for 3 hours topping up the water as necessary. Turn out on to a dish and serve with custard. Serves 3–4.

During and after the Napoleonic Wars many service officers were forced to live for periods, sometimes quite extended, on half pay; hence the popularity of this simple and substantial pudding.

Golden syrup can be substituted for black treacle but the pudding will then lack the authentic 'Christmas Pudding' flavour.

Yarmouth Harbour by A. Heaton Cooper

Winkle Street, Calbourne by A. Heaton Cooper

ISLE OF WIGHT PIES

½ lb. shortcrust pastry
2 medium eggs
4 oz. granulated sugar
4 oz. butter
2 oz. ground rice
1 teaspoon ground nutmeg
Halved glacé cherries

Set oven to 375°F or Mark 5 and grease patty tins. Roll out the pastry thinly on a lightly floured surface, cut into rounds and use to line the patty tins. Prick the bottom of each with a fork. In a bowl, beat together the eggs and sugar until the mixture is thick and frothy. Melt the butter in a pan until just liquid, add the ground rice and the nutmeg, and lastly the egg and sugar mixture. Mix well together and half-fill each patty tin with the mixture. Place half a cherry on each pie and bake for about 15 minutes or until golden brown. Turn out on to a wire rack and leave to cool. These pies keep well. Makes about 15–18 pies.

White Soup

2 oz. butter
2 lb. potatoes, peeled and cut into chunks
1 large onion, peeled and finely chopped
4 sticks celery, wiped, trimmed and finely chopped
1½ to 2 pints chicken stock
3 sprigs parsley, 1 sprig thyme and a bay leaf, tied together
Salt and black pepper
1 pint milk
1 dessertspoon cornflour
A little fresh, finely chopped parsley for garnish

Melt the butter in a large saucepan, add the potatoes, onion and celery, cover and cook for 5 minutes. Add the stock, herbs and seasoning, bring to the boil, then cover and simmer for 1 to 1½ hours. Allow to cool slightly, remove the herbs and blend thoroughly in a liquidiser. (If a *really* smooth consistency is required, run the liquidised soup additionally through a sieve.) Return the soup to a clean saucepan, add the milk and bring to the boil. Blend the cornflour with a little water to form a smooth paste and stir into the soup. Heat through thoroughly and adjust the seasoning if necessary. Pour into soup bowls and serve garnished with chopped parsley and accompanied by croutons. Serves 4 to 6.

Ventnor from Steephill Walk by E. W. Haslehust

Ryde – Moonrise by A. Heaton Cooper

Rice Cake

4 oz. butter, softened
Finely grated rind of a lemon
8 oz. caster sugar
4 oz. flour
4 oz. ground rice
4 eggs

Queen Victoria was a devotee of afternoon tea and Rice Cake was one of her favourite cakes.

Set oven to 350°F or Mark 4. Cream the butter and lemon rind together, then beat in the sugar until the mixture is light and fluffy. Sift the flour and fold in, then fold in the ground rice. Separate the eggs and beat the yolks into the mixture, one at a time, mixing thoroughly. Whisk the egg whites until they stand up in soft peaks and fold carefully into the mixture. Spoon into a lined and greased 8 inch cake tin (round or square) and bake for 1 to 1¼ hours, covering the top with kitchen foil if browning too quickly. Cool in the tin for 5 minutes, then turn out on to a wire rack. If baked in a round tin, dust the top with sifted icing sugar and serve whole. If baked in a square tin, allow to get completely cold then cut into squares, dusting with sifted icing sugar. This cake is quite moist and slightly crunchy in texture.

Vectis Pudding

8 oz. prepared suet pastry
4 oz. black treacle
1½-2 oz. currants or sultanas
1 cooking apple, peeled, cored and chopped
Grated rind of half a lemon
½ teaspoon mixed spice

Roll out the suet pastry on a lightly floured surface to form a strip 8-10 inches long. Spread the treacle to within 1 inch of the edges, then arrange the fruit on top. Sprinkle with lemon rind and mixed spice and roll up from the long side, and seal the edges well with a little milk or water. Roll up in a clean, floured pudding cloth and tie the ends – but leaving room for the pudding to swell. Steam for 2 hours, topping up the water as necessary. Serve the pudding cut into slices and accompanied by cream or custard. Serves 4-6.

If preferred, golden syrup can replace the black treacle, though this is not traditional to the recipe.

Alum Bay and the Needles by W. W. Quartremain

Bembridge Harbour by E. W. Haslehust

Bramble Dessert

8 oz. blackberries, hulled and washed
2 medium cooking apples, peeled, cored and finely sliced
2 oz. sugar
1 teaspoon lemon juice
4 oz. fresh brown breadcrumbs
3 oz. soft brown sugar
¼ teaspoon ground cinnamon
3 oz. butter
Whipped cream to decorate

Place the blackberries, apple, sugar and lemon juice in a saucepan and stew gently until the fruit is soft but still holds its shape, adding a little water, if necessary. Allow to cool. Mix together the breadcrumbs, brown sugar and cinnamon. Melt the butter in a frying pan, add the breadcrumb mixture and stir well until crisp and golden. Allow to cool. Layer the fruit and the breadcrumb mixture in a glass serving dish, starting with the fruit and finishing with the breadcrumbs, and chill thoroughly. Serve decorated with rosettes of whipped cream, and accompanied by pouring cream. Serves 4 to 6.

Brown George Pudding

4 oz. fresh white breadcrumbs
1½ oz. flour
½ teaspoon bicarbonate of soda
2½ to 3 oz. soft brown sugar
3 oz. finely shredded suet
1 egg
4 oz. black treacle
Milk

In a bowl, mix together the breadcrumbs, flour and bicarbonate of soda and then stir in the sugar and suet. Beat the egg into the treacle and stir into the mixture with sufficient milk to make a soft, dropping consistency. Turn into a well buttered 2 pint pudding basin, covering the top with a piece of greased greaseproof paper and a piece of kitchen foil. Tie down and steam for 2½ to 3 hours, topping up the water as necessary. Turn out the pudding on to a warm serving dish and serve with warmed treacle and cream or custard. Serves 4 to 6.

The Hanoverian Georges were particularly fond of rich steamed or boiled puddings, hence the name of this Isle of Wight pudding in which 'Brown' refers to its colour.

If preferred golden syrup can be substituted for the black treacle, though this is not traditional and the resulting pudding will not be as brown.

Carisbrooke Castle by C. Essenhigh Corke

Totland Bay by A. Heaton Cooper

A Solid Syllabub

½ pint medium sherry
4 oz. sugar
1 pint double cream
A little grated nutmeg
The rind and juice of a lemon

Pour the sherry into a bowl. Grate the lemon rind finely and add to the sherry. In a separate bowl pour the lemon juice over the sugar and stir well. Add to the sherry and continue to stir until the sugar has dissolved. Whip the cream until it stands up in soft peaks and fold into the sherry mixture. Spoon into 4 sundae glasses and then sprinkle the tops lightly with nutmeg. Keep in the refrigerator until served. Serves 4.

This was a popular Victorian dessert recipe.

PRINCE ALBERT'S PUDDING

4 oz. sugar
4 oz. butter, softened
2 eggs, beaten
4 oz. flour
¼ teaspoon baking powder
Pinch of salt
6 oz. raisins
1 oz. candied peel, finely chopped
2 teaspoon ground mace
A little milk, if necessary

In a bowl, cream the sugar and butter together until light and fluffy, then beat in the eggs. Sift together the flour, baking powder and salt and fold into the egg mixture, then add the raisins, peel and mace, adding a little milk if the mixture seems too stiff. Spoon the mixture into a well buttered 2 pint pudding basin, cover with lightly buttered greaseproof paper and kitchen foil and tie down. Steam for 1½ to 2 hours, topping up the water as necessary. Turn out on to a warmed serving dish and serve accompanied by pouring cream or custard. Serves 4 to 6.

Whippingham Church by A. Heaton Cooper

Shanklin Head by W. W. Quartremain

Almond Cake

9 oz. unsalted butter
8 oz. sugar
4 eggs, beaten together
8 oz. flour
1 oz. ground almonds
1 oz. ground rice
1 teaspoon baking powder
Pinch of salt
4 tablespoons dry sherry
3 or 4 drops almond essence
A little sifted icing sugar

Set oven to 350°F or Mark 4. Cream the butter and sugar together until very light and fluffy and beat in a little of the eggs. Sift the flour, ground almonds, ground rice, baking powder and salt together and fold into the creamed mixture alternately with the remainder of the beaten eggs. Stir in the sherry and the almond essence. Spoon the mixture into a well greased and lightly floured 8 inch round cake tin and bake for 1¼ hours, covering the top with kitchen foil if it appears to be browning too quickly. Cool in the tin for 5 minutes, then turn out on to a wire rack. Before serving, dust the top of the cake lightly with the sifted icing sugar.

SLOE OR 'KIXSIES' JELLY

Sloes
Water
Sugar

Wash the sloes, put them into a saucepan and cover with water. Bring to the boil and simmer until the fruit is thoroughly soft. Turn the fruit out into a jelly bag or fine cloth and strain, squeezing when cool enough to handle. Measure the juice into a preserving pan or large saucepan and add 1 lb of sugar to every pint of juice. Heat gently until the sugar is dissolved, stirring continuously, and then bring to a rolling boil until the jelly thickens. Test for setting on a cold plate. When setting point is reached pour into sterilised jars, cover and seal. The jelly is a very rich, dark colour and has a sharp invigorating flavour.

Kixsies is the local Isle of Wight name for sloes.

Shalfleet by A. Heaton Cooper

Marine Parade, Cowes by W. W. Quartremain

Wootton Steamed Pudding

2 eggs and their weight in sugar
and butter
3 oz. flour
1 teaspoon baking powder
Marmalade

Grease a 1 pint pudding basin. In a bowl, cream together the sugar and butter. Mix the baking powder with the flour and stir into the creamed mixture. Separate the eggs and beat the yolks together. Stir the yolks into the mixture and add a large tablespoon of marmalade. Whisk the whites of the eggs well together and mix in thoroughly. Turn into the greased pudding basin and cover with kitchen foil, making a pleat to allow for expansion. Steam for 2 hours. Turn out the pudding and top with additional marmalade. Serves 4.

Blackberry Roll

8 oz. blackberries, hulled and washed
1 medium cooking apple, peeled, cored and finely chopped
3 oz. raisins
6 oz. sugar
1 teaspoon ground cinnamon
1 teaspoon lemon juice
2 tablespoons water
A small 'walnut' of butter
2 oz. flaked almonds
8 oz. shortcrust pastry
Beaten egg or milk to glaze

Place the fruit, sugar, cinnamon, lemon juice, water and butter in a saucepan and simmer, stirring frequently, until the mixture has thickened to a marmalade-like consistency. Cool, then stir in the almonds. Set oven to 400°F or Mark 6. Roll out the pastry on a lightly floured surface to form a neat rectangle and brush *very* lightly with beaten egg or milk. Allow to dry, then spread the fruit mixture over to within approximately half-an-inch of the edge of the pastry. Roll up carefully, like a Swiss Roll, seal the edges well, then brush with beaten egg or milk to glaze. Place on a lightly greased baking sheet and bake for 25-30 minutes or until golden brown. Serve, sliced with cream or custard. Serves 4.

Vectis Doughnuts

6 oz. flour
½ teaspoon baking powder
2 oz. butter
2 oz. sugar
1 large egg, beaten
Strawberry jam
Lard or oil for frying

Sieve together the flour and baking powder into a bowl, then rub in the butter until the mixture resembles fine breadcrumbs. Mix in the sugar, add the beaten egg and mix to a stiff paste. Roll out the pastry on a lightly floured surface to about 3/16"–1/4" thick and cut into rounds with a 2 inch cutter. Place a little knob of jam in the centre of half of the rounds, moisten the edges and cover with the remaining rounds; press the edges firmly together. Fry in deep fat until golden brown, taking care not to overheat the fat; lard gives a better flavour. Turn out, drain on kitchen paper and place on a wire rack to cool. Makes about 8–10 doughnuts.

METRIC CONVERSIONS

The weights, measures and oven temperatures used in the preceding recipes can be easily converted to their metric equivalents.

Weights

Avoirdupois	Metric
1 oz.	just under 30 grams
4 oz. (¼ lb.)	app. 115 grams
8 oz. (½ lb.)	app. 230 grams
1 lb.	454 grams

Liquid Measures

Imperial	Metric
1 tablespoon (liquid only)	20 millilitres
1 fl. oz.	app. 30 millilitres
1 gill (¼ pt.)	app. 145 millilitres
½ pt.	app. 285 millilitres
1 pt.	app. 570 millilitres
1 qt.	app. 1.140 litres

Oven Temperatures

	°Fahrenheit	Gas Mark	°Celsius
Slow	300	2	140
	325	3	158
Moderate	350	4	177
	375	5	190
	400	6	204
Hot	425	7	214
	450	8	232
	500	9	260

Flour as specified in these recipes refers to Plain Flour unless otherwise described.